YOLANDA FERNANDEZ

Affiliate Marketing for Beginners

The Ultimate Guide To Earning Online

Contents

1

Introduction

Welcome to "Affiliate Marketing for Beginners: The Ultimate Guide to Earning Online." If you're eager to explore the world of making money online but don't know where to start, you're in the right place. This book is your gateway to understanding affiliate marketing—a straightforward and powerful way to generate income without complex technicalities.

In the following pages, we'll break down affiliate marketing into bite-sized, easy-to-understand pieces. You don't need prior experience or a tech-savvy background to embark on this journey. All you need is the willingness to learn and the desire to succeed.

Affiliate marketing offers you the chance to earn a passive income by promoting products or services you believe in, without the need to create your own. Whether you dream of quitting your 9-to-5 job, want to supplement your current income, or simply seek financial freedom, this guide will provide you with the foundational knowledge and practical steps to get started.

We'll take you through the basics, from understanding what affiliate marketing is to selecting your niche, creating a website (if you want one), and joining affiliate programs. You'll learn how to effectively promote affiliate products, track your success, and navigate common challenges.

But this guide isn't just about the "how-to" of affiliate marketing; it's also about the "why." You'll discover how ethical practices, building trust with your audience, and staying compliant with regulations are keys to long-term success in this field.

So, if you're ready to embark on an exciting journey towards financial independence and explore the world of affiliate marketing in a clear, concise, and easy-to-follow manner, let's dive in. Together, we'll demystify affiliate marketing and set you on the path to achieving your online income goals.

2

Understanding Affiliate Marketing

I magine earning money online without creating your own products, handling customer service, or investing in complex business infrastructure. That's the magic of affiliate marketing, a concept so simple that anyone can grasp it.

What Is Affiliate Marketing?

At its core, affiliate marketing is a partnership between you (the affiliate) and a company or merchant. You promote their products or services, and when someone buys through your unique affiliate link, you earn a commission. It's like being a digital middleperson, connecting buyers with products they're interested in.

How Does Affiliate Marketing Work?

1. Joining an Affiliate Program: You start by signing up for an affiliate program. Many companies offer these programs,

making it easy to find products or services in your area of interest.

2. Getting Your Unique Affiliate Link: After joining a program, you receive a unique affiliate link. This link tracks the people you refer to the company's website.

3. Promoting Products or Services: Next, you promote the products or services using your affiliate link. This can be done through various online channels like websites, blogs, social media, email, or YouTube.

4. Earning Commissions: When someone clicks on your affiliate link and makes a purchase, you earn a commission. Commissions can vary, but they're typically a percentage of the sale or a fixed amount.

The Key Players: Affiliates, Merchants, and Consumers

- Affiliates: That's you! You promote products or services as an affiliate marketer.

- Merchants: These are the companies or individuals who offer affiliate programs. They provide the products or services and handle sales, customer service, and order fulfillment.

- Consumers: These are the people who buy through your affiliate links. They're looking for solutions to their problems or fulfilling their desires, and you help them find what they need.

The Affiliate Marketing Ecosystem

- Affiliate marketing operates within a vast online ecosystem. Here's a simplified view of how it all fits together:

- Affiliate Networks: These are platforms that connect affiliates (you) with multiple merchants. They simplify the process of finding and joining affiliate programs.

- Content Creators: These are individuals who create content on various online platforms. They can be bloggers, YouTubers, Instagram influencers, or anyone with an online presence.

- Online Shoppers: These are people searching for products or services online, often looking for reviews, recommendations, or information before making a purchase.

- Affiliate Managers: Some larger affiliate programs have dedicated managers who assist affiliates, answer questions, and provide resources to help them succeed.

In this chapter, you've taken your first steps into the world of affiliate marketing. You've learned what affiliate marketing is, how it works, and who the key players are. Now, let's move on to the exciting journey of finding your niche, a crucial step towards your success as an affiliate marketer.

3

Finding Your Niche

In the world of affiliate marketing, choosing the right niche is like picking the perfect fishing spot. It's where you'll focus your efforts, and the choice can significantly impact your success. In this chapter, we'll explore why selecting a niche is crucial and guide you through the process.

The Importance of Choosing a Niche

Imagine trying to be everything to everyone. It's an exhausting and ultimately futile endeavor. The same principle applies to affiliate marketing. Here's why choosing a niche matter:

1. Expertise: Focusing on a specific niche allows you to become an expert in that area. You can provide valuable information, answer questions, and gain the trust of your audience more effectively.

2. Targeted Audience: A niche narrows down your audience to people genuinely interested in what you offer. This means

higher conversion rates and more satisfied customers.

3. Less Competition: In a broad market, you'd compete with countless affiliates. In a niche, you face less competition, making it easier to stand out.

Researching Profitable Niches

To choose a niche wisely, you need to consider its profitability. Here's how to research and evaluate potential niches:

1. Passion and Interest: Start with your interests and passions. What topics excite you? Remember, you'll be spending time creating content, so it should be something you enjoy.

2. Market Demand: Research whether there's a demand for your chosen niche. Use tools like Google Trends, keyword research tools, or social media trends to gauge interest.

3. Competition Analysis: Assess your potential competitors. Are there already successful affiliates in your chosen niche? While competition isn't a bad thing, it's essential to understand your competition and find a unique angle.

4. Monetization Potential: Consider how you can monetize your niche. Are there affiliate programs or products you can promote within this niche? Look for products or services that offer reasonable commissions.

Identifying Your Target Audience

Understanding your target audience is key to affiliate marketing success. Here's how to define your audience:

1. Demographics: Consider factors like age, gender, location, and income level that describe your ideal audience.

2. Psychographics: Dive deeper into their interests, values, and behaviors. What problems or needs do they have that your niche can address?

3. Content Preferences: Learn how your target audience consumes content. Do they prefer reading blog posts, watching videos, or engaging on social media?

4. Challenges and Pain Points: Identify the problems your audience faces within your niche. Your content should provide solutions and answers.

By narrowing down your niche and understanding your target audience, you're laying a solid foundation for your affiliate marketing journey. In the next chapter, we'll explore how to create your online presence, whether it's a website, blog, or social media platform, to start connecting with your audience and promoting affiliate products effectively.

4

Setting Up Your Online Presence

Now that you've chosen your niche, it's time to establish your online presence. Your online platform will serve as the hub for your affiliate marketing efforts, allowing you to connect with your target audience and promote affiliate products effectively. In this chapter, we'll explore the essential steps to get you started.

Creating a Website (or Blog)

Having a website or blog is a powerful way to showcase your expertise, provide valuable content to your audience, and promote affiliate products. Here's how to get started:

1. Choose a Domain Name: Select a domain name that reflects your niche and is easy to remember. Use domain registration services to secure your chosen name.

2. Web Hosting Basics: Sign up for a reliable web hosting service. Look for one that offers good uptime, customer support, and

9

scalability as your website grows.

3. Website Design and Content Strategy: Keep your website design clean and user-friendly. Organize your content logically, and plan your content strategy to provide value to your audience.

Choosing a Domain Name

Your domain name is your online address, so choose it wisely. Here are some tips:

- Keep it short and memorable.
- Use relevant keywords if possible.
- Avoid special characters and complicated spellings.
- Check for domain name availability before settling on a name.

Web Hosting Basics

When selecting a web hosting service:

- Consider your budget and the hosting provider's pricing plans.
- Look for good uptime and reliability.
- Check for scalability to accommodate future growth.
- Read user reviews and consider customer support responsiveness.

Website Design and Content Strategy

A well-designed website is essential for creating a positive user experience. Here's how to approach it:

- Choose a clean and mobile-responsive design.
- Organize your content logically with clear navigation menus.
- Plan your content strategy to address the needs and interests of your target audience.

Website vs. Blog

While a blog is a type of website, it focuses primarily on content publication. Blogs are excellent for building trust and authority within your niche, but they require consistent content creation. A traditional website, on the other hand, may be more suitable if you plan to offer various types of content or services.

In this chapter, we've covered the fundamental steps for creating your online presence, whether it's a website or a blog. Your online platform will be the cornerstone of your affiliate marketing business, allowing you to engage with your audience and promote affiliate products effectively. In the next chapter, we'll delve into the crucial process of joining affiliate programs, which is the gateway to earning commissions as an affiliate marketer.

5

Joining Affiliate Programs

With your online presence established, it's time to dive into the heart of affiliate marketing—joining affiliate programs. These programs are the bridge connecting you to the products or services you'll promote and the commissions you'll earn. In this chapter, we'll explore the ins and outs of affiliate programs and guide you through the process of getting started.

Affiliate Networks vs. Independent Programs
Before we jump into the process of joining affiliate programs, it's essential to understand two primary types of affiliate programs:

1. Affiliate Networks: These are platforms that bring together affiliates (you) and multiple merchants in one place. They simplify the process of finding and joining programs, tracking your earnings, and receiving payments. Some popular affiliate networks include ShareASale, ClickBank, and Amazon Associates.

2. Independent Programs: Some companies run their own affiliate programs without going through an affiliate network. These programs can offer unique advantages but may require more effort to find and join.

Popular Affiliate Networks

To get started, consider exploring these widely recognized affiliate networks:

- Amazon Associates: Ideal for beginners, as it offers a vast array of products and a trusted brand.

- ShareASale: Known for its wide variety of affiliate programs across different niches.

- ClickBank: Focuses on digital products like e-books and software, often offering high commissions.

- CJ Affiliate (formerly Commission Junction): Features a broad range of affiliate programs from well-known brands.

Applying to Affiliate Programs
Once you've chosen an affiliate network or identified independent programs of interest, here's how to apply:

1. Create an Account: Sign up for an account on the affiliate network's website or the merchant's affiliate program page.

2. Provide Necessary Information: Fill out your profile information, including your website URL and payment details.

3. Browse and Apply: Search for affiliate programs within your niche. When you find one that aligns with your content and audience, click on "Apply" or "Join Program."

4. Approval Process: Some programs approve affiliates automatically, while others may require manual approval. Be patient during this phase.

5. Affiliate Dashboard: Once approved, you'll gain access to your affiliate dashboard. Here, you can find your unique affiliate links, promotional materials, and track your earnings.

Getting Approved: Tips and Strategies

To increase your chances of being approved by affiliate programs:

- Have a well-established online presence, such as a professional website or blog.

- Ensure your website has high-quality content relevant to the affiliate program's niche.

- Be honest and transparent about your promotional methods and audience.

- Comply with program-specific requirements and policies.

In this chapter, we've covered the crucial step of joining affiliate programs, whether through affiliate networks or independent programs. Now that you're part of affiliate programs, you're ready to start promoting products or services to your audience. Chapter 5 will guide you through the various methods of effectively promoting affiliate products, helping you maximize your earnings as an affiliate marketer.

6

Promoting Affiliate Products

Congratulations! You've taken the first steps to becoming an affiliate marketer by joining affiliate programs. Now, it's time to dive into the exciting world of promoting affiliate products effectively. In this chapter, we'll explore various methods to connect with your audience and encourage them to make purchases through your affiliate links.

Content Creation Essentials

At the heart of successful affiliate marketing lies valuable content. Whether you run a blog, website, or social media platform, your content should inform, engage, and persuade your audience. Here's how to create content that converts:

1. High-Quality Content: Ensure your content is well-researched, informative, and free from errors. Quality content builds trust and authority.

2. Relevant Keywords: Use relevant keywords related to your

niche in your content. This helps your content rank higher in search engines and reach a broader audience.

3. Engaging Headlines: Craft compelling headlines that grab your audience's attention and entice them to read further.

4. Visuals: Incorporate images, videos, and infographics to make your content more engaging and visually appealing.

SEO Basics for Affiliates

Search Engine Optimization (SEO) is the practice of optimizing your content to rank higher in search engine results. Here are some fundamental SEO principles for affiliate marketers:

1. Keyword Research: Identify the keywords your target audience is searching for and incorporate them naturally into your content.

2. On-Page SEO: Optimize your content's titles, headings, and meta descriptions to make it more search-engine-friendly.

3. Quality Backlinks: Build high-quality backlinks to your content from reputable websites within your niche.

4. User Experience: Ensure your website is user-friendly, with fast loading times and mobile responsiveness.

Leveraging Social Media

Social media platforms are powerful tools for affiliate marketers to connect with their audience and promote affiliate products.

Here's how to make the most of social media:

1. Choose the Right Platforms: Identify the social media platforms where your target audience spends the most time.

2. Engage Authentically: Build relationships with your followers by engaging in conversations, responding to comments, and providing value.

3. Share Valuable Content: Share not only affiliate promotions but also informative and entertaining content relevant to your niche.

4. Use Affiliate Links Wisely: Disclose your affiliate relationships and use shortened, user-friendly affiliate links.

Email Marketing for Affiliate Success

Building an email list is a valuable asset for affiliate marketers. Here's how to effectively use email marketing:

1. Build Your List: Encourage visitors to subscribe to your email list by offering valuable incentives like e-books, newsletters, or exclusive content.

2. Segmentation: Segment your email list based on subscribers' interests and behaviors, allowing you to send targeted affiliate offers.

3. Provide Value: Balance promotional emails with valuable content, tips, and recommendations to keep subscribers engaged.

4. Clear Calls to Action (CTAs): Use clear and compelling CTAs in your emails to encourage clicks and conversions.

By combining these content creation, SEO, social media, and email marketing strategies, you'll be well-equipped to promote affiliate products effectively. In the next chapter, we'll delve into the importance of tracking and analytics, helping you measure your affiliate marketing efforts' success and make informed decisions for optimization.

7

Tracking and Analytics

In the world of affiliate marketing, knowledge is power. To succeed, you need to understand what's working, what's not, and how you can improve. That's where tracking and analytics come into play. In this chapter, we'll explore the importance of monitoring your affiliate marketing efforts and using data-driven insights to optimize your strategy.

The Importance of Tracking

Imagine setting out on a journey without a map or GPS. You might eventually reach your destination, but it will take much longer and be far less efficient. Tracking is your map in the affiliate marketing world. It helps you:

1. Measure Success: Track your affiliate links to see which ones are driving conversions and earning commissions.

2. Identify Weaknesses: Pinpoint areas where your strategy may be falling short, such as low conversion rates or high bounce

rates.

3. Optimize Campaigns: Use data to make informed decisions and optimize your campaigns for better results.

Setting Up Tracking Tools
To effectively track your affiliate marketing efforts, you'll need some essential tracking tools:

1. Google Analytics: A free and powerful tool that provides insights into website traffic, user behavior, and conversion rates.

2. Affiliate Network Tracking: Most affiliate networks offer tracking tools within their platforms. These tools provide data on clicks, conversions, and commissions for each affiliate link.

3. URL Shorteners: Services like Bitly or Pretty Links allow you to create short, branded links that are easier to manage and track.

4. Conversion Tracking: Implement conversion tracking pixels or codes on your website to track specific actions, such as form submissions or purchases.

Analyzing Data for Optimization
Once you've set up tracking tools, it's time to analyze the data they provide. Here's how to make sense of your affiliate marketing analytics:

1. Click-Through Rate (CTR): Measure the percentage of people

who clicked on your affiliate links. A higher CTR indicates that your audience is interested in the promoted products.

2. Conversion Rate: This metric tells you the percentage of clicks that resulted in a sale or desired action. A higher conversion rate is a sign of a successful campaign.

3. Earnings and Commissions: Track your earnings and commissions to understand which affiliate products are the most profitable.

4. Traffic Sources: Analyze where your website traffic is coming from. This helps you focus your efforts on the most effective channels.

Making Informed Decisions
Data-driven decisions are the cornerstone of successful affiliate marketing. Here's how to use the insights you gain from tracking and analytics:

1. A/B Testing: Experiment with different strategies, such as changing your content, CTA buttons, or promotional methods, and compare the results.

2. Content Optimization: Identify your top-performing content and replicate its success in future campaigns.

3. Adapt and Evolve: Stay flexible and willing to adapt your strategy based on what the data tells you.

4. Budget Allocation: Allocate your time and resources to the

most effective campaigns and channels.

Tracking and analytics empower you to refine your affiliate marketing strategy continuously. In the next chapter, we'll explore the various ways you can monetize your affiliate marketing business and diversify your income streams for long-term success.

8

Monetizing Your Affiliate Business

Congratulations on your journey through affiliate marketing! By now, you've learned how to choose your niche, create an online presence, promote affiliate products, and analyze your efforts. In this chapter, we'll explore the various ways to monetize your affiliate business, maximize your commissions, and ensure long-term financial success.

Diversifying Income Streams

One of the key principles of financial stability in affiliate marketing is diversification. Relying on a single income source can be risky. Here are some ways to diversify your income streams:

1. Promote Multiple Products: Instead of relying on one affiliate product, explore and promote various products or services within your niche. This reduces the impact of fluctuations in one product's performance.

2. Explore Different Affiliate Programs: Join multiple affiliate

programs or networks to expand your options and revenue potential.

3. Create Your Products: As your expertise and audience grow, consider creating and selling your own products, such as e-books, courses, or merchandise.

4. Offer Services: Leverage your knowledge and skills to offer consulting, coaching, or freelance services related to your niche.

Maximizing Commissions

To maximize your affiliate earnings, consider the following strategies:

1. Focus on High-Commission Products: Prioritize products or services that offer higher commissions. However, ensure they are relevant to your audience.

2. Cross-Selling: Recommend complementary products or services alongside your primary affiliate offers to increase the average transaction value.

3. Upselling: Promote higher-priced versions or add-ons of the products you're affiliated with to earn more per sale.

4. Long-Term Strategies: Invest time in building evergreen content that continues to generate commissions over time.

Scaling Your Business

As your affiliate marketing business grows, you can scale it to reach a broader audience and increase your income. Here's how:

1. Outsource and Delegate: As your workload increases, consider outsourcing tasks like content creation, SEO, or social media management to free up your time for strategy and growth.

2. Expand Your Product Range: Continuously research and add new affiliate products or services to your portfolio to cater to evolving market trends and audience needs.

3. Build a Team (When Ready): If you're managing a significant affiliate marketing operation, consider hiring team members to assist with various aspects of your business.

4. Plan for Long-Term Success: Develop a long-term business plan with clear goals and milestones. Regularly review and adjust your plan as needed.

Avoiding Common Pitfalls

While affiliate marketing can be profitable, it's not without its challenges. Here are some common pitfalls to avoid:

1. Over-Promotion: Avoid bombarding your audience with affiliate links. Maintain a balance between valuable content and promotional content.

2. Lack of Transparency: Always disclose your affiliate relationships to maintain trust with your audience.

3. Ignoring Compliance: Familiarize yourself with legal regulations and compliance guidelines, especially the Federal Trade Commission (FTC) rules, to avoid legal issues.

4. Impatience: Affiliate marketing success often takes time. Don't get discouraged if you don't see immediate results.

In conclusion, monetizing your affiliate business involves diversifying your income streams, maximizing commissions, scaling your efforts, and avoiding common pitfalls. By following these principles, you can build a sustainable and profitable affiliate marketing business over the long term.

9

Staying Compliant and Ethical

As you navigate the world of affiliate marketing, it's crucial to operate within the boundaries of legal and ethical practices. Compliance and ethics not only ensure the longevity of your affiliate marketing business but also build trust with your audience. In this chapter, we'll explore the importance of staying compliant and ethical in affiliate marketing.

Understanding FTC Guidelines

The Federal Trade Commission (FTC) in the United States has established guidelines to protect consumers and maintain transparency in affiliate marketing. Key points to consider:

1. Disclosure: You must clearly disclose your affiliate relationships to your audience. This can be done with phrases like "This post contains affiliate links" or "I may earn a commission if you purchase through my links."

2. Transparency: Be honest and transparent about your experiences with the products or services you promote. Avoid making false claims or endorsements.

3. Unbiased Reviews: If you provide reviews, they should be unbiased and based on your genuine experiences with the product or service.

4. Material Connections: Disclose any material connections you have with the product or service provider, including free products, sponsorships, or affiliate relationships.

Building Trust with Your Audience

Trust is the foundation of successful affiliate marketing. Here's how to build and maintain trust with your audience:

1. Provide Value: Offer valuable content, whether it's informative articles, honest reviews, or helpful recommendations.

2. Transparency: Be open about your affiliate relationships and disclose any potential conflicts of interest.

3. Avoid Deceptive Practices: Do not engage in deceptive practices, such as fake reviews or misleading advertising.

4. Quality over Quantity: Prioritize quality over quantity. It's better to promote products you genuinely believe in rather than chasing commissions.

Ethical Affiliate Marketing Practices

To maintain your ethical standards in affiliate marketing, consider these practices:

1. Product Knowledge: Only promote products or services you're knowledgeable about and genuinely believe can benefit your audience.

2. Audience Alignment: Ensure that the products you promote align with your audience's needs, interests, and expectations.

3. Honest Reviews: If you provide reviews, present both the pros and cons of the products or services. Your audience will appreciate your honesty.

4. Continual Learning: Stay updated on industry trends, ethical guidelines, and legal regulations related to affiliate marketing.

Handling Negative Feedback

Not everyone will be satisfied with the products or services you recommend. When you receive negative feedback or complaints:

1. Listen and Respond: Listen to your audience's concerns and respond respectfully and professionally.

2. Problem Resolution: If a promoted product has issues, work with the merchant to resolve them. Your reputation is at stake.

3. Transparency: Be transparent about any product shortcomings and what steps you're taking to address them.

In conclusion, staying compliant and ethical in affiliate marketing is essential for long-term success. It builds trust with your audience, helps you avoid legal issues, and ensures your reputation remains positive. By following ethical practices, you can create a sustainable affiliate marketing business that benefits both you and your audience.

10

Troubleshooting and Problem Solving

I n the dynamic world of affiliate marketing, challenges are bound to arise. However, with the right strategies and a problem-solving mindset, you can navigate these hurdles effectively. In this chapter, we'll explore common issues affiliate marketers encounter and provide practical solutions to address them.

Dealing with Declining Sales

Problem: You notice a drop in your affiliate sales, and commissions are dwindling.

Solution:

1. Analyze Your Content: Review your content to ensure it's up to date and relevant. Update and refresh older posts to maintain their appeal.

2. SEO Check: Perform an SEO audit to see if your content is still

optimized for relevant keywords. Adjust your content strategy as needed.

3. Explore New Products: Consider promoting different products or services within your niche. Market trends change, and diversifying your offerings can help.

4. Engage Your Audience: Connect with your audience through surveys, social media, or email. Ask for feedback and determine what products or content they're interested in.

Handling Affiliate Program Changes

Problem: The affiliate program you've been promoting changes its terms or commission structure.

Solution:

1. Stay Informed: Regularly check for updates from the affiliate programs you're part of. Subscribe to their newsletters or follow their blogs.

2. Assess the Impact: Analyze how the changes will affect your earnings and strategy. Adjust your promotional efforts accordingly.

3. Explore Alternatives: If the changes are unfavorable, explore other affiliate programs or products within your niche.

4. Negotiate: In some cases, you can negotiate terms with the program manager, especially if you have a strong track record

as an affiliate.

Managing Technical Issues

Problem: Technical glitches on your website or with tracking tools are affecting your affiliate marketing efforts.

Solution:

1. Regular Maintenance: Schedule regular maintenance for your website to ensure it functions smoothly. Consider professional website monitoring services.

2. Tracking Tools: If your tracking tools are malfunctioning, contact the affiliate network's support team for assistance.

3. Backup Plans: Have backup plans in place, such as using alternative tracking methods or affiliate links, to mitigate disruptions.

4. Tech Support: Seek assistance from technical experts or developers if issues persist.

Staying Motivated and Persistent

Problem: Maintaining motivation and consistency can be challenging in affiliate marketing, especially during slow periods.

Solution:

1. Set Clear Goals: Define achievable short-term and long-

term goals for your affiliate marketing business. Having a clear purpose can keep you motivated.

2. Stay Informed: Continuously educate yourself about industry trends and strategies to keep your passion alive.

3. Celebrate Small Wins: Acknowledge and celebrate even small achievements. Recognizing your progress can boost motivation.

4. Network and Collaborate: Connect with other affiliate marketers or industry peers for inspiration, collaboration, and shared experiences.

Remember that challenges are a part of the affiliate marketing journey. By staying persistent, adaptable, and proactive, you can overcome these hurdles and continue building a successful affiliate marketing business.

In the final chapter, we'll discuss strategies for scaling your affiliate marketing business and taking it to the next level, whether it's through outsourcing, expansion, or long-term planning.

11

Conclusion

Congratulations on completing this guide to affiliate marketing for beginners! You've gained valuable insights into the world of affiliate marketing, from selecting your niche to building an online presence, promoting products, and troubleshooting common issues. Now, as you embark on your affiliate marketing journey, let's recap the key takeaways and encourage you to take action.

Key Takeaways:

1. Choose Your Niche Wisely: Select a niche that aligns with your interests and audience's needs, and conduct thorough research to ensure its profitability.

2. Build Your Online Presence: Create a website, blog, or social media platform to connect with your audience and establish yourself as an authority in your niche.

3. Join Affiliate Programs: Explore affiliate networks and

independent programs, and apply to those that resonate with your niche and audience.

4. Promote Ethically and Transparently: Always disclose your affiliate relationships, provide honest reviews, and prioritize your audience's interests.

5. Track and Analyze: Use tracking tools and analytics to measure your success, make data-driven decisions, and optimize your strategies.

6. Diversify and Maximize Earnings: Explore multiple income streams, maximize commissions, and scale your business as it grows.

7. Stay Compliant and Ethical: Adhere to FTC guidelines, maintain transparency, and build trust with your audience through ethical practices.

8. Troubleshoot Effectively: Address challenges like declining sales, program changes, technical issues, and motivation with practical solutions.

Taking Action:

Now that you've acquired the knowledge and tools, it's time to take action. Start by setting clear goals for your affiliate marketing business, whether it's generating a side income, achieving financial freedom, or launching a thriving online career.

Remember, success in affiliate marketing often requires patience and persistence. Stay committed to providing value to your audience, keep learning, and adapt to evolving trends and technologies.

As you navigate your affiliate marketing journey, don't forget that challenges are opportunities for growth. Embrace them with a problem-solving mindset, and you'll find that each hurdle brings you closer to your goals.

Thank you for choosing "Affiliate Marketing for Beginners: The Ultimate Guide to Earning Online" as your companion on this exciting adventure. We wish you every success in building a profitable and fulfilling affiliate marketing business!

12

Additional Resources

In your affiliate marketing journey, you'll encounter a wealth of resources that can further enhance your knowledge and skills. Here's a list of valuable resources to explore:

1. Affiliate Marketing Networks:

- [ShareASale](https://www.shareasale.com/): A popular affiliate marketing network with a wide range of programs.
- [ClickBank](https://www.clickbank.com/): Known for its digital products, ClickBank offers high commission rates.

2. Affiliate Marketing Tools:

- [Google Analytics](https://analytics.google.com/): A powerful tool for tracking website traffic and user behavior.
- [SEMrush](https://www.semrush.com/): Provides SEO and

competitive analysis to enhance your content strategy.

3. Legal and Compliance Resources:

- [Federal Trade Commission (FTC)](https://www.ftc.gov/): The official website for FTC guidelines and regulations.
- [FTC Endorsement Guides](https://www.ftc.gov/tips-advice/business-center/guidance/ftcs-endorsement-guides-what-people-are-asking): Specific information on endorsement disclosures.

4. Email Marketing Services:

- [MailChimp](https://mailchimp.com/): A popular email marketing platform to help you build and manage your email list.

5. Social Media Groups:

- Facebook and LinkedIn host various affiliate marketing groups where you can connect with fellow marketers, ask questions, and share insights.

These resources offer a wealth of information and support to help you succeed in your affiliate marketing endeavors.

Remember that continuous learning and staying up-to-date with industry trends are key to long-term success. Explore these resources and tailor your learning journey to your specific needs and goals.

13

Disclaimer

The information provided in this book, "Affiliate Marketing for Beginners: The Ultimate Guide to Earning Online," is for educational and informational purposes only. While every effort has been made to ensure the accuracy of the content, the author and publisher make no representations or warranties of any kind regarding the completeness, accuracy, reliability, suitability, or availability of the information contained within.

The techniques, strategies, and tips discussed in this book are based on the author's knowledge and experiences. The affiliate marketing landscape is dynamic, and industry trends, guidelines, and regulations may change over time. Therefore, readers are encouraged to independently research and verify information, guidelines, and compliance requirements relevant to their specific affiliate marketing activities.

The author and publisher of this book are not responsible for any actions taken by readers based on the information provided herein. Affiliate marketing involves financial and legal considerations, and readers are advised to seek professional advice, when necessary, especially in areas related to compliance, legal regulations, and financial decisions.

The use of any product, service, or recommendation mentioned in this book should be done with careful consideration of individual circumstances and at the reader's own risk. The author and publisher shall not be liable for any losses, damages, or injuries arising from the use or misuse of the information provided in this book.

By reading this book, you acknowledge and agree to the terms of this disclaimer. It is your responsibility to use the information presented in this book responsibly, in compliance with applicable laws and regulations, and in a manner that aligns with your personal and professional goals.

If you find this book helpful, I'd be very appreciative if you left a favorable review for the book on Amazon!